Earth Tones:
A Journey

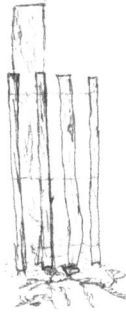

Poetry for the Journey

Gary W. Burns

Turning Corner Books ™

WWW.TURNINGCORNERBOOKS.COM

Other Books of Poetry
by Gary W. Burns

Bridges: To There
(Poems for the Mind, Body & Spirit)

Clouds: On the Wind
(Poems for the Soul – A Meditation)

Garden Walks: Hand In Hand
(Poems To Relax By)

Moments: This to the Next
(Poetry - Now and Eternity)

Poems of Love: A Selection

Rainy Day: Wondering
(Poems for a Rainy Day)

To You With Love: Selected Poems

Twilight: Awaking the Stars
(Poems of the Night's Light)

To Ewurabena

*for her love
of the rain*

೫ ——————————— ೫

CONTENTS

⌘ For The Telling

i

⌘ Along The Way

⌘ Wave After Wave

⌘ Sojourn

For the Telling

Off Folly Beach
South Carolina

March 4th, Days End

On
For as far
As my eyes can see
Run the clouds
And they, slowly moving,
Shower down colors
Arrayed in pastel.

I see the pink
Calling to crimson
Over there where
Tomorrows' sun
Is vanishing
From today.

Now
With the sun gone
Night-black
Makes its way
Through sunset gray.

So ends
The day.

Morning

Rays
Of yellow-gold
Sent
By stories old

Telling of light;

Morning.

The Wonder
Of It All

Spring came
In her gentle gender
And bore me a summer
I'll always remember.

We were lovers
Her and I.

Entwined with her
While walking by the sea
I watched her paint
Destiny;

O what artistry.

Love Eternal

How wonderful the spring
In which we watched
The early tulips bloom
And the robins
Hurry about the yard
As a late snow
Came down:

Love eternal.

21 June,
The Rain

This is what
 I've been waiting for

The rain's
Falling with ease
Not storm,

Watering the flowers
Tenderly;

Two lovers meet.

Decisions

Love,
Being blind,
Appears to be curl
And at the same time
Kind.

Some live pleased
Others pine.

Angel-like

How does an Angel
Make its way

I know

Because

I'm watching you
And that's the way
You
Make your way too

Be

The heavens call
To you and me

Eternally

Be

Not Alone

We're not alone,

For as the moon
Shares the stars
With the sky

We share I
With all's that by

Be it low
High
Far or nigh

Here and Now

Our time here
          is short.
Come near.
Let me hold you.

Please.

A Venetian Sketch

Off in the fog
A gondola
Rest,
A hazy figure.

It glides away.

Quickly
It's hidden
In Venetian-gray.

Carefree
Endlessly

O these days of
The blue-sky-breeze,
Clouds that please,
Butterflies
Sailing carefree
On greenery
And life
Filled to bream
With beauty.

Ah
Carefree
Endlessly . . .

The Circle
Of Holding

Let love
Take you
And
Warm arms
Make you
Whole

In the circle
Of holding.

Listening

You call it
Coincident

I call it
Heaven sent,

Listen . . .

Without End

We are all secrets
Told

With out end . . .

Rainbows

1

The storm
Not subsiding

Struck
Harder
Releasing
Pelting rain

Everything
Bent
And bowed
To the blustery wind

2

Make it
Through the storm

And the rainbow
Is won

You'll see

Come on

Arm In Arm

1

The sun
Is still
High in the sky
And has
A long way to go
Till setting.

So,
Arm in arm,
Let's go
Together
Along this stretch
Of the day.

2

We'll tell one another
The story
Of our journey;

The wants, the needs
The almost.

And, perhaps, tell
Of how some dreams
Came true
And how others
Are still
In their dreamy sleep.

3

The sun's still
So high in the sky.

Let's go along
Together,
Arm in arm,
And share
Our story.

Along the Way

Highway 24 W
Kentucky

Nameless

Each a beating heart
Of Love:

Namelessly,
The children go running
To the water's edge

Then plunge
Into the ocean
Called . . .

At Morning's Edge

1

The edge of morning looms
          in the cool depths
               of a deep purple
As the night's streetlight eyes
          go out
               one-by-one.

2

Last night,
          in a sea
            of people and ebony,
Nothing moved quickly
          to my
             searching eye.
There were pairs of legs
          dangling in aisles
And the bus and train rides
          found me
            wanting to find you,
               and I did.
The night's good for
          finding and loosing.

3

But the night's lost too,
    for in a sudden
     flush of rose,
      the skyline yawns
      the morning dawns
And all's a memory
            or not.

Before Goodbye

1

You won't always
Hold me.

I know
Someday,
You'll go away.

But, for now,
For this day,

Before good-byes

Let's be
Not you, nor me
But one
With Love.

2

Let's give
What love
Wills us to give.

Let's kiss
In the sweet mist
Of love.

Let's embrace
And without haste
Allow our very souls
To be
Ecstasy.

Before you go
Let's know

One Love.

All Day Long

Love
Wins the day

Be Love

In Earth Tones: A Journey

Toronto

Thank you
For coming to find me.

I saw you there
Talking
Among the people
Who were moving about
That afternoon
On Young Street.

My shyness
Kept me only looking.

Then you found me.

That afternoon together,
That evening,
And the next evening too.
Filled with love
And you.

Often
You are thought of.

                    With Love,
                    Yours always

Peaceful Hills

Clouds, lazily,
Come over the hills.

Summer,
Stretching
Along the little valley,
Yawns.

And the wonder of it all
Sings
In all things.

Loving Arms

How open
Can open be

That's
How open
My arms are

Waiting

To hold you

In Love

You and I

Moments
Spontaneous

Dressed
In motion

Dancing
on and on
and on . . .

In Love

In Earth Tones: A Journey

Sundance

While standing
Beside
The millers' pond;

Sunshine droplets
Showering down
Dance
On waters wind-cresting.

We

No I
Is singular

No you
Is without me

Flexible

Branches dance
Easily in the wind

They *live*
And *give*
In the bend

Stay flexible

To Riyadh

I've seen deserts before
But none like this

For-ever-on
Sand and sand,
Smooth horizons
Unfolding
Smooth horizons

A sea of wind
Without time
A heat that defies
The meager shade

A place
Where may be seen
A world still ferried
Atop the ancient camel

Magnificent

Healing

It's okay.

No matter what,
Sing your song.

As each day
Opens its arms

Fall in love
Again ,
And again,
And again.

It
Is

Seeming
To come, then go
Then, come again

But always

Whether here
Or gone

It
Is

The gold
Of the Golden Rain tree

Content

The raindrops,
Content with falling,
Have filled the pond.

And now,
The water rolls gently
Over the spillway
A lot like you
Rolling to your side
Gently,
Content.

Harmony

From within
The dark night

Shines

Light

In Earth Tones: A Journey

Sorrow

A bird
At sea, in the rain
Needs to fly
Just the same

Wave After Wave

Nanakuli Beach
Hawaii

From Love
And Me

Now that the leaves
Have fallen
From the trees
I can see the hills
Not the masquerade
Of canopy.

This is what the years
Have done for me.

Over time I've learned
The truer sense
Of love.
And I've learned
The wonder of giving.

I listen now
And by some grace
Somehow
I discern the voice
Of sincerity.

              Warmly,
              Love and Me

Each of Us

A flickering flame

Naked
In the rain

Known as time

Free

The days
Will go by

Let them

And be . . .

Ever So

1

It's a gusty day
In late November.

2

The clouds are dark.

3

A late fallen leaf, auburn,
With a tinge of brown,
Swept to the ground
To tumble round,
Has stumbled past
My park bench view.

4

It's now made its way,
Or perhaps,
The way was made
For it,
Be what may,
It's now in the pond
With the geese.

5

Ever so,
Life
Makes its way.

6

A chilly November rain
Is just over the ridge.
It's sprinkling.

7

From the sprinkles
Come the rains
Then sun
And shine.

The Winds
And Change

1

While watching
The winds of change
Make their way
On a windswept day

I looked up
To see

A vast horizon
Unfolding
Before me.

2

Then it was, somehow,
The down turn of this
And the down turn of that,
So ready to cover up the day,
Went away.

3

And as fresh winds blew
I found myself anew
And lovingly free
To be me.

Green Leaves

We age
Not as fine wine
Or as jewels
Finely set
But
More like
Leaves
Green
Then yellowed
Then browned
Then whisked
To the ground

The silent
Sound
Of round

Make Ready

With the advent of day
We made way.
Setting sail
There came a gale.

No time was lost,
No spare of cost,
Us seafarers
Made ready as best
Ready could be
In such a sea.

The Alps,
A Day Trip

I'm glad we didn't calculate
The trip to the mountains
In hours and distance.

Departing
And having only thoughts
Of love
The grand valleys,
The marvelous dales,
The far-off-snow-pecks
And the lowlands scenery
Came into focus
With a charm
Deserving of it all.

Lying here
Upon the hillside
Watching the clouds
Make their nomadic-way
Across the valley
I hear
The cool mountain wind
Rushing
Over your soft skin.

Night's Fallen

I feel good
When night
Is not near
But about me:
When shadows
Live within shadows
And my midnight view
                    is of you.

Till I'm Deep
In Sleep

Hold me
Release me

Then
Hold me
Once again

Don't let go

Hold me

Till I'm deep
In sleep.

The Canvas

Be it together,
Apart,
At the end,
Midpoint,
Or start;

We live
Intertwined
Upon
The canvas
Life.

The Ancients

The ancients
Were wise

But,
Not the wisest.

The wisest

Are yet to come.

Along Journeys' Way

Let's laugh,
Love,
Live,

Let's take
Only to give,

Let's sing
Love songs,

Our journey
Begins

Seasons Pass

There are red
    and golden leaves
Which have yet to fall
    from the trees.

It's not quite rain,
    not quite fog.

Flowers fade away,
Quietly
    settling their debt,
The bargain for the bloom.

Words

Sounds
Rushing by;
The brook.

In Earth Tones: A Journey

Unlock Your Heart

1

Locked hearts
Can't get past the point
Where love begins
And loneliness ends.

Unlock your heart
For me
Please.

2

Open it up
Come out
Let's talk, then
Let me in.

3

You'll begin
To know
The warmth
Of love.
And
By loves eternal flame
See the world
All aglow.

Unlock your heart
For me
Please.

1 AM

It's 1 AM
And winter's dark
Shrouds my window
Cloaking hues
And concealing
    snowy views.

But out
Under the heavenly stars

Night's
A delight
Lit by starlight.

Thank You

It's as if
I've newly found
The ease
With which
The gentle breeze
Blows
Through the trees.

The warm wind
Soft,
The yellow sun
Caressing;

A moment

Forever.

Every day's
So wonderful
Since I found you.

Thank you.

What of Eternity

We can't walk paths
In any direction
But what they lead,

Count any more stars
Then what there are,

Or see
Any farther
Than sight.

But,
If paths
Go on and on,
If stars
Are all of light,

And if sight sees
Endlessly

Eternity
May be

You and me.

Not Leading
Nor Following

Not leading,
Nor following

In all of your going

Go

In the name of Love

Sojourn

Off Highway 10
Arizona

Whether Within
Or Without

Some people
Make their world
Within
Watchfully
Looking out.

Others,
Make the world
Without
Within
And there begin
To live.

Nonetheless,

Whether
Living within
Or
Living without
You are with Love
Let there be
No doubt.

Your Own Way

1

I enjoy
   our conversations.

I know
   we live
      busy lives
  rushing everywhere
Ending up
    no-where
      different
And somehow
    always
       being here.

2

I understand
　　　your days
　　　　are filled
　　　　　with living
And your nights
　　　　with dying
　　　　　to dream
　　　　　　of days
　　　　　　　filled
With even
　　　more living.

I am grateful
For our conversations.

I understand
　　　you need to go

Your own way.

Dear Old Po,

A note to say: I see winter's
knocking on late autumn's door.

Leaves, styled in colorful dress,
Have, for a time now, been
parading about. Meanwhile,
the gray flannel-clad-fog has been
making itself known about the hills.

There's not much blue in the sky
these days and the foggy-gray
easily gives away the plot
of the play.

2

I believe, I'll leave till noon
the frosty calling card
left at my mailbox last evening.
For certainly, by then
it will be gone.

Of late, as night falls,
I'm sung to sleep now and again
by the singsong of early winter rains.

But then again, at times,
my eyelids are brought down
by the soft whispers of calm winds.

3

   By the way Dear Old Po,
there's one rose still thinking
summer or spring. It's the brightest
of reds. Standing so proud against
the brown grass and gray-dappled
day; its blush warms me.

4

  Gone the crickets' cadence-song;
gone the colorful flower scenery.

  But I feel somehow
dear old wine loving Po
all of this you surely know.

Humbly yours,

As December Sleeps

1

Let's let
December sleep
Under its snowy
Blanket.

We owe it that.

It's been busy
All year
Making its way
To here.

2

But let's keep
Tonight awake
Stirring
And moving
In give
And take.

Sleep can come
After love
Has done
All it will.

Let's let
December sleep
Deep
But keep

Tonight
Awake
For us.

Sunrise
Sunset

If I had but one vista
To view
Just one
I could see

And the choice
Were left to me

The sight would be

The sun going down

That I may share
In its forever rising
As we go round
And round
And round

Deep Winter

Quiet,
Revealer of serenity;
Bliss
For you and me.

Endlessly

Each instant,

Love endlessly.

ABOUT THE AUTHOR

Inspired by nature and the beauty around him
Gary W. Burns started writing poetry at a young age.
Early on Gary was able to express his thoughts, ideas
and emotions through the vivid imagery of his verse.
His poetry has been published in various literary arts
journals, anthologies and magazines. He is the author
of 10 books of poetry. Through his poems Gary
shares his reflections on the many facets of life and
on the beauty of nature. The expressiveness of his
poetry has been enriched by his wide reading in
philosophy and psychology. He has traveled
throughout the world and has lived in numerous
countries, to include, Italy, Korea, Saudi Arabia and
Canada. He has also lived in Hawaii and several
other states. Currently, Gary makes his home in
Northern Virginia near the foothills of the Blue Ridge
Mountains

ENJOY THESE OTHER BOOKS OF POETRY BY GARY W. BURNS

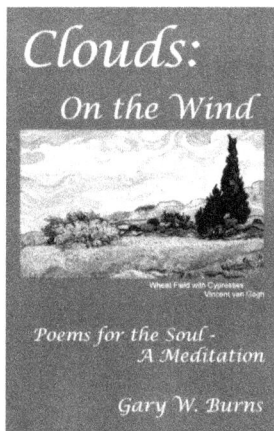

Clouds: On the Wind
(Poems for the Soul - A Meditation)
ISBN: 978-0-9845342-0-2 (Paperback)
ISBN: 978-0-9845342-1-0 (Hardcover)
ISBN: 978-0-986090-3-5 (E-Book)

Bridges: To There
(Poems for the Mind, Body & Spirit)
ISBN: 978-0-9827805-6-5 (Paperback)
ISBN: 978-0-9827805-7-2 (Hardcover)
ISBN: 978-0-9860900-4-2 (E-Book)

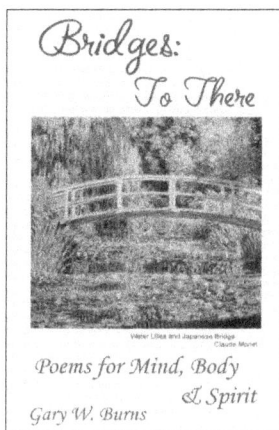

Garden Walks: Hand In Hands
(Poems to Relax By)
ISBN: 978-0-9845342-3-4 (Paperback)
ISBN: 978-0-9827805-0-3 (Hardcover)
ISBN: 978-0-9860900-1-1 (E-Book)

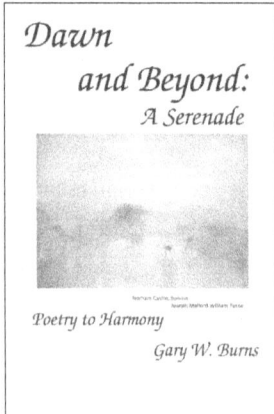

Dawn and Beyond: A Serenade
(Poetry to Harmony) (Due Out)
ISBN: 978-0-9827805-8-9 (Paperback)
ISBN: 978-0-9827805-9-6 (Hardcover)

Moments: This to the Next
(Poetry - Now and Eternity)
ISBN: 978-0-9845342-4-1 (Paperback)
ISBN: 978-0-9827805-1-0 (Hardcover)
ISBN: 978-0-9860900-9-7 (E-Book)

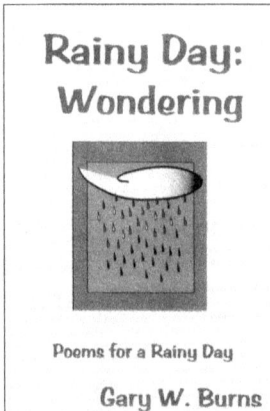

Rainy Day: Wondering
(Poems for a Rainy Day)
ISBN: 978-0-9845342-5-8 (Paperback)
ISBN: 978-0-9827805-2-7 (Hardcover)
ISBN: 978-0-9860900-7-3 (E-Book)

To You With Love: Selected Poems
ISBN: 978-0-9845342-6-5 (Paperback)
ISBN: 978-0-9827805-3-4 (Hardcover)
ISBN: 978-0-9860900-2-8 (E-Book)

Twilight: Awaking the Stars
(Poems of the Night's Light)
ISBN: 978-0-9845342-7-2 (Paperback)
ISBN: 978-0-9827805-4-1 (Hardcover)
ISBN: 978-0-9860900-6-6 (E-Book)

Poems of Love: A Selection
ISBN: 978-0-9845342-8-9 (Paperback)
ISBN: 978-0-9827805-5-8 (Hardcover)
ISBN: 978-0-9860900-5-9 (E-Book)